Octaves

John Watson

Octaves

A Paris Labyrinth

Acknowledgements

Almost all the characters in this Montparnasse pageant were real. They are amply documented in many sources, including Billy Kluver, *Kiki's Paris: Artists and Lovers 1900–1930*; William Wiser, *The Crazy Years*; Humphrey Carpenter, *Geniuses Together*; and John Glassco, *Memoirs of Montparnasse*. Here may be found many of the anecdotes on which these poems depend.

Octaves
ISBN 978 1 76041 489 4
Copyright © text John Watson 2018

First published 2018 by
Ginninderra Press
PO Box 3461 Port Adelaide 5015 Australia
www.ginninderrapress.com.au

A Barge Offshore

One autumn morning Kisling rose.
Two models who had stayed the night
Were still asleep, like dreaming cats.
He washed. He breakfasted on pears,

And smiled to see the bed in shade,
A barge which on its tousled deck
Bore strewn profusion to the shore.
In sunlit wash it docked. They woke.

Pascin at Work

Sketching incessantly, Pascin
Sat at the Dôme, still in his hat,
His chin supported in his hand,
With cigarette as periscope.

They brought more paper with his wine.
He'd tint the page with coffee grounds
Or pigment dropped into a schnapps –
All round his chair rose crumpled mounds.

In Fontainebleau

The heads of trees of crème de menthe,
And over them the clouds the sun
Is forming, and against that bank
The eucalypts, irregular

And zany, branch above the hedge.
A path shines like Excalibur.
This landscape honours Bonnard's words:
'Let it be felt the painter was here.'

Kiki Impersonates

She seized a jaunty sidelong hat,
And thrust one hand into her dress
To imitate Napoleon.
She raked her skirt above her thighs

Whose full and splendid white might seem
Napoleon's breeches. 'Sirs! Mesdames!'
The barman said, 'I give you now
The brandy of the self-same name.'

Per Krohg Meets Lucy

'When first I saw her in the pool' –
He drained another glass to raise
The pyramid of glasses – 'There,
She stood in light against the sun.

She seemed a palm tree in the breeze
Or slow subsiding parachute
But then in blazing sun through cloud,
A twin-legged table bearing fruit.'

Kiki Poses

She entered very quietly,
Her little finger at her mouth.
She seemed about to laugh aloud
Then took her coat off and was nude.

(A piece of coloured handkerchief
Pinned at the throat implied a dress.)
It seemed the sun had come upstairs
And stood there striving to impress.

Kisling to His Models

'The splendours of the world surpass
Whatever might be made of them.
It's dusk. Put on some clothes. We'll walk,
And raise a glass to fading light;

We'll celebrate this turning world
And irreversibility,
Who hold the streamers left behind
By liners now far out to sea.'

A Bugatti Parked by the Bridge

A perfect summer's day. Derain,
In driver's cap, sat at the wheel,
An apple on the dashboard, leaves
And shadows blurred above the screen,

The hills in folds ruched round the stream.
They left the car to be refuelled.
A table spread with bread and fruit
Looked like a painting of a field.

In Youth Is Pleasure

As bees kiss clover, Kiki moved
From one affection to the next,
Always with laughter, which it seemed,
Became her partner as she danced.

As Kiki's laughter filled the Dôme
Her dancing seemed to turn the world –
While Lenin tried to lose at chess
Against Apollinaire, and failed.

Sunbathing

Pascin had wandered far upstream.
He walked across the weir. The sound
Persisted in the long canal
Down to the estuary, where birds

In squalls around the fishing fleet
Drowned out the distant weir. Sun lace
Filled all the sky where Kiki lay,
Her petticoats across her face.

Ancient Mode

He crossed and then recrossed the weir.
Kiki was bathing in the sun,
The lapping shallows at her feet.
The sky seemed drained of time. The world

Was like a fractured hour-glass, and
This beach its sand. Intrigued, Pascin
Observed, all day, the day observe
Melismas echoing Leonin.

Photograph

Pascin with permanent cigarette;
Foujita smiling scrutably;
Unknown woman; Ezra Pound
Half ill at ease; Jane Heap with glass.

They watch the dancers on the floor
Where, flowering like a vine in shade,
A pretty girl completely nude
Dances unnoticed in the crowd.

Spillway

Nothing else was moving then.
The world had come to rest its gaze
With chin cupped in supporting hands.
The water fell as if it rose.

Derain made pebbles skip. Pascin
Was wading in the circling pool
In shadow where the spillway hung,
Like Chinese silk caught in a spool.

Desnos Relates a Dream

'The hiking tour set out across
High country split by a ravine.
At length, entering this gorge, we reached
The Present, on a painted sign.

The narrow path ran through a gate
Which stood half open. And, at once,
We were led on. We longed, instead,
To spread across that valley floor.'

In the North

One day when strange, volcanic clouds
Camped out along the line of hills,
Per Krohg and Lucy pitched their tent
Amongst the tundra's heated springs.

The wind blew every way it would.
Diffracted light came down like sleet;
It almost seemed the day had plans
To wander on into the night.

Their Romance Blossoms in Greenland

The land which Eric Bloodaxe named
So verdantly to influence
The hopeful traveller from the south
Now spread serenely, grey and calm.

Per Krohg and Lucy wandered there;
Directionless it led them on
Like modulating harmonies
In Schubert or Jerome Kern.

Kiki Refutes Plato

Someone had scrawled across the wall,
'Abstraction underpins the world,
Whereby an image bodies forth
Ideas which must always remain

Potent but unattainable.'
Against such rhetoric Kiki's smile
Appeared to offer willingly
Without a trace of cant, the Real.

Bronia and Tylia

The god's high hall fell strangely hushed,
The earth was trembling, trees knelt down,
The steep sky soundless. In the west,
Winds sank, the ocean stood becalmed,

And Jupiter himself was still.
Two nymphs were dancing at the Dôme,
Oblivious, serene. Crowds gazed
As if the air were honeycomb.

Man Ray Sets Out

He woke up in the darkroom, dawn
In some mysterious way announced.
And, later, when he'd shaved and left,
The morning like a lover's smile

Singled him out. The reckless day
Was swaying on the pavement. Light
Gushed from the hydrant. And, in white,
Kiki was waiting to be met.

First Meeting

From holding hands at the cinema
Where light's tall stories charmed the gloom,
Man Ray brought Kiki home to see
His darkroom in its amber light.

Next, she undressed behind a screen
Rehearsing early signs of love.
He put aside his camera
And drew the shades in Plato's cave.

Kiki's Letter

Kiki had come to pose, but when
She came out from behind the screen
Their lips met and the afternoon
Saw no more photographs. Kiki wrote,

'I watch you work in that red glow
And wait for you on your divan:
I bite your mouth until it bleeds,
Your KikiwhoadoresyouMan.'

The Duchess Regrets

In moiré rooms by candlelight
The memory of sleepless nights
When Proust, to calm his asthma, might
Drink seventeen black coffees… Now,

The world has left that world behind.
When no one listens she must make
The orchestra play the same piece twice,
Then ask guests, 'Which one did you like?'

Tableau Vivant

When Bronia and her sister came
From lands below the sea held back
From flood by dykes, to Montparnasse,
Bronia, sixteen, met Radiguet.

Who could foretell that in a year
That Tithonus would die, and she
Would pose as Cranach's naked Eve
For New Year's grave festivity?

An Ideal Agenda

A cool wind fanned the terraces,
Announcing dawn. And to his friends,
Still lingering over more champagne,
Kisling spoke more expansively,

'I want life to be beautiful,
And women granted their desires,
The day to take its shape from them
And happiness to grow on trees.'

Questionnaires

Researchers for a magazine
Gave questionnaires to Kisling's friends.
Their published answers flattered him.
Per Krohg, 'He likes blondes and brunettes

And every colour in the world.'
Dardel, 'A sheep in wolf's disguise.'
'I'll have to whisper in your ear,'
(Kiki). 'Beware. Avert your gaze.'

Kisling Observes Bronia

'She has the silence of a room
Which looks out on a teeming lake
Where nesting swallows swerve and cry.
And even here, despite the band,

The crowded floor, the dancers' noise,
She seems to watch from such a place.
She's modelled for me many times
And yet I've never caught that face.'

Further Attempts at Description

When Bronia danced with Radiguet
'Mysterious beauty' took the floor.
From somewhere near the orchestra
Was heard, '…that apprehended form

Which floats below the melody
In Schubert's final year of grace,
Invisible and everywhere –
And there you have pale Bronia's face.'

Foujita Proposes

The fountains froze, arresting time
In which Fernande would welcome him.
It must have been the way she swung
The Louis Quinze chair through the air

To break it up and feed the fire…
Or was it the whiteness of her arm?
For without further thought he spoke
And asked her would she marry him.

Summer Evening

The rower's arrow moves upstream
Against the pointed paths of birds
Which fly towards the estuary.
In silver evening lanes, the light

Is muffled. Kiki, though, is not.
The shower of rain has passed. She runs,
And, shedding garments as she goes,
Scatters the seagulls on the lawns.

The Painter of the *Demoiselles* Rebuked

'We first met, sheltering from the rain;
He brought me to his tousled bed.
But now, five years have passed. I'm bored.
I'm bored with cats and keeping house,

But worst of all, he's cruel to me,
By keeping from me things he reads.
On Sundays (when we should be close),
He hides *the Katzenjammer Kids*.'

View of the Lake at Sunset

A strange west wind of almost-spring
Made all the ferrous cliffs see red;
The cirrus clouds were amber stained
As if the world must rust away.

Beneath these clouds' crème caramel,
Derain's Bugatti came to rest,
Its fender at the cliff. He waved:
'My friends, behold the Golden West.'

The Artists' Ball

Foujita won, to much acclaim,
The medal of the *Légion d'Honneur*
By painting only landscapes, nudes,
And only women with short hair.

The Artists' Ball at Montparnasse
Saw honour lodged where it was due:
He pinned it to his fancy dress –
A strongman's loincloth in blue.

Wide-eyed

Then Kiki to sustained applause
Sang 'Smoke Gets In Your Eyes'. All saw,
Wide-eyed, her eyelids' painted eyes
Which vanished as she opened them.

Foujita passed this compliment,
'She's tall and unexpected as
Tree dahlias pale amongst bamboo.
She's on my mind. I'm on my knees.'

The Confidence of Foujita

Foujita, in the boulevard
Beneath the double chestnut rows,
Saw women turning, looking up,
All with Louise Brooks' burning gaze

Which burned like fire in Plato's cave.
Supremely confident, alone
In all that shadow-casting crowd,
He found himself invited in.

Lucie Badoul Becomes Youki

Lucie lay reading, in her bed,
Apollinaire's *La Femme Assise*.
'I leapt from bed, put out the cat,
Put on my makeup, took the train

To Montparnasse. I knew no one.
Some poets spoke to me. I saw
Foujita seated in a bar.
The forest of my heart lay bare.'

At the Jockey

When laughing Kiki danced, she wore
Loose underskirts and, it was clear,
Nothing beneath them. When she sang,
She sang the words which Desnos wrote,

Half-sleeping at the raucous bar,
Who, when he'd covered one serviette,
Would call for more – for wistful songs
Of true love mingled with regret.

Blissful Dancing

A tree was reaching out, the sky
Was casting wide its net, the rain
Was calculating when to fall,
Pale evening came, ingratiating –

All were seeking similes,
Except for Kiki and Man Ray
Who had no need for likenesses,
And danced the summer night away.

The Coming Out of Hermine

At twenty-one, Hermine David
Was sewn into her clothes. But soon
Her mother's fears were realised:
Pascin, with scissors in his hand.

Hermine now wore geranium red;
And thenceforth Pascin drew her nude
In blurred ink wash and shadowy line,
As if she flowered in his shade.

In the South

Stained, like the belly of a mole
Dappled in areas, smooth and bare,
The curving winter hillside hunched
And huddled at the suckling stream.

Hermine and Pascin stopped to stare;
Formless as Balzac's dressing gown
Seemed all this floating, other world,
Away from cafés and the town.

Kiki's Unusual Sunset

'Look!' cried Kiki at the crest.
The plain lay under golden light.
The Seine extended in a curve
And glimmered like a smile. She said,

'It's just as if the villagers
Had put down sheets, and hour on hour
Were harvesting those saffron threads,
The stamens of the crocus flower.'

Another View of the Valley

Cloud shadows crossed the valley floor
Like pebbles rolling in a stream.
The air was warm. She watched these wraiths
Against the sounds of distant birds.

Kiki was leaning from the cliff.
'They're like a cat walking across
A balcony,' she said, and laughed
To hear the echoes of her voice.

La Ruche, the Beehive

Soutine each evening left La Ruche,
'A kind of architectural Brie
Each portion starting with a point
And ending in a window,' thence

To the drawing class and samovar
To drink tea from a saucer, cooled
And sucked in through a lump of sugar,
'Like light brought to this sombre world.'

The Origins of the Beehive

The Queen of Romania paid Boucher
To make La Ruche, a studio
For artisans and artists,
With caryatids and details from

The Paris Exposition. Thus
The Queen (and Queen of Dreadful Verse
As Carmen Sylva) gave the world
A nectar cell, a working space.

A Challenge

The alstroemerias' speckled throats
Throw out this challenge: find another
Substance in the physical world
To match our blazoned silk-pink. Soon,

Flamingoes, watermelons stir;
But then, above the clover hill,
The clamorous sunset claims the prize.
And Kiki plucks a roseate spill.

Dusk

The time it took the sun to set
Between entanglement in trees
And final calm, with nesting birds,
Lucy was walking by the lake

And pondering these imponderables:
The blackbird's sweet and touching cries,
And how, in this oceanic world
Love can persist through waves of days.

Breasts

Kisling had made a partial list
To celebrate his models. So,
'The hill far from the valley floor,
The melon, the arrow under silk,

And (this preferred by Errol Flynn),
The twin diverging ski-jump course…
They vary as these blossom trees
Which press themselves through winter's dress.'

Spring

The tree-lined streets seem overfilled
With branches waving, brandishing
Their flowering library of leaves.
The blandishments of spring have come.

Kiki approaches through their fans,
Her make-up like her floral dress,
Eyes on her eyelids, painted lips,
All brought to challenge spring's excess.

After a Late Night Kisling Rises Early

A tightness in the world assumes
Something akin to glistening.
As if the light were packed and coiled,
It springs loose in the firmament,

The way a tree-fern first unfolds.
A concentrated landscape aches.
He wakes from early morning sleep.
The parsley world unfolds. He works.

On the Generosity of Victor Libion

Libion, invited for a meal,
Saw instantly the furnishings,
The glasses, cutlery and plates,
And even chairs, were from his bar.

He left and soon returned with wine:
'Good friends, I thought you might like this,
One thing I'd not provided. Now
Let's eat. I'm hungry as a horse.'

The Wave

One wave amongst the rest which rose
Against the lime-green wooded shore
Was symbolist. It hung like hair
Across a naiad. In the sky

Auroras burned. This Hokusai
Seemed not to move, a fluted hem
Of coral folds. Try as he would
Pascin could not quite capture them.

Desnos Sees Yvonne George at the Olympia

Five-pointed star, the pentagram,
The star-fish, swimming point on point,
Turned like a windmill in the swell,
He chose as her emblem. So, he swam,

Five senses all obsessed by her,
His star, lodestar with violet eyes
Like the evening star at dusk.
This passion lasted five starred years.

Caryatids

'Pascin now rose, and raised his glass.
"I want you all to come tonight
To my studio. We'll celebrate
Whatever you would celebrate."

We went inside. As one might place
A vase of flowers against the wall
He had arranged on a divan
Two naked twin girls, rouged and pale.'

Desnos Wakes from a Dream of Days

The slight and subtle differences
Between the light at noon and two;
And then, at four, such puzzlement:
How have these changes all occurred,

While all the while, at any time,
A changelessness appears to bloom?
Clear water in the hourglass,
The year cascading through the room.

Desnos Sees *The Winter's Tale*

He watched in breathless happiness
The statue scene where one, thought dead
And living on in what seemed stone,
Stepped slowly from that pedestal.

He found himself beside himself,
Both selves as statuesque as hers
Before she breathed and moved and sighed
And stepped down to the world's applause.

Desirable Kitsch

The Kisling nude with potted palm
Is confident and vacuous,
Modigliani's girl next door
Or woman shopping in Printemps

With poodle on a gilded chain.
She stretches on her silk divan,
Smiling, expensively undressed
And gazes from a magazine.

Life and Times of Arthur Cravan, Poet and Boxer

'But craven Arthur? Never! Though
Jack Johnson floored him in the sixth,
This was, as everyone agrees,
Because a verb clung to a noun.

And when he married Mina Loy
And went to Rio and his grave,
Lost overboard, it was in search
Of some elusive adjective.'

A Defence

Discussing Schubert in the bar
Someone exclaimed, 'Look! Even now
A monoplane appears outside,
Roses stand in a glass of wine,

The valley greets a fall of snow…
And, even so, you criticise,
Despite such unexpectedness,
His "undeveloping ideas".'

Recollections of a Lady from the Sphinx

'Cezanne made weekly visits here.
The girls surrounded him with smiles
He seemed always the fruiterer
At market choosing apples, pears.

We laughed a lot – he was a dear –
And yet beneath a gas lamp there
I felt it strange to be transformed
Into a cone, a cube, a sphere.'

Stormy Weather

One sultry afternoon Desnos
Saw, on the cyclorama sky,
Two weathers meet, divided by
A sharp ruled line in blurring ink,

On one side darkening cumulus clouds
And, on the other, fields of light.
Crossing that line, he saw himself
With Yvonne George, his star, his fate.

Spring's Burgeoning

The last snows gone, the Seine resumes
Its careless flood past Notre Dame.
The trees put out new leaf. Again
Despite their variousness, each thing

Is pressed by old familiars.
Man Ray and Kiki, arm in arm,
Feel cells within them fret, protest
At having to preserve their form.

Paintings by Kiki; Preface by Desnos

Desnos wrote these affectionate words:
'You have, my dear, such beautiful eyes,
The world you see through them must be
As beautiful. What do you see?

A grassy field in some calm glade,
Beside a curved, contented sea;
That valley is your Paris. Here
You see the night as sun-filled day.'

Life in the Hive

When Boucher walked out with Jeanette,
His donkey, in the cluttered grounds
To circumambulate La Ruche
And came upon milk-thistles there

(A special treat, like dusk or fruit),
Soutine was indoors painting meat;
Others put paintings out of reach
Of Soutine's spattered overcoat.

Per Krogh and Lucy

A tree by Corot leaned across
Their path. Flowers grew at their feet –
The wild white violet. The stream
Merged with the cries of birds, as if

Communications might resume
Between all creatures. In all this,
They saw, like banners on the trees,
Signs of their future happiness.

Their Wedding

The guests still putting on their coats
Approach the church along the lane,
While one who seems absurdly tall,
Her dark dress shimmering, sheds a tear.

Outside the church, through fields of flowers
With wooden swings like boats, blithely
Derain's Bugatti stops. Out steps
The bride, a gauze anemone.

Othello, Act V

'One afternoon at Jimmy's Bar
We met a student of the Bard,
A painter of his favourite cat.
He asked us home. We stayed till late.

At length he put the cat outside.
It ran back in, clung to the mat…
Again he tried, and mused, "Put out
The cat and then put out the cat."'

A Remedy

Sometimes when afternoon in flower
Had turned to seed and fallen, so
Kiki grew sad. Sometimes the day
Had modulated to a key

So inexplicably remote
That Kiki found herself alone
And falling out of love. What then?
Play 'Dinah' on the gramophone.

Formative Experience

Young Pascin at the Turkish baths
With ancient aunts saw, every day,
Revealed, 'the conscientious nude'
(Thus Henry James on Bougereau).

Years later Pascin came of age,
And wearied of Reality:
'Truth, always naked, without lace,
No longer stirs the blood in me.'

A Metaphysical Restaurant

'You mean,' she said, 'that we should eat
Once more from that forbidden tree
In order to fall back again
Into a state of innocence?'

The waiter said, 'I couldn't help
But overhear you then. That course
Of which you speak, is, I believe,
Today the Specialty of the House.'

Kiki Reading Aloud from a Poiret Brochure

Kiki wore yellow. 'Should Rosine
Wake pensively, she must choose green,
The myrtle, shade of mystery;
Should jealousy shine like a sun,

Nasturtiums' orange will agree;
If treacherous, the peonies' red;
And jonquil yellow only when
Desire returns her to her bed.'

Kiki Continues in Poiret's Mellifluous World

'Like light held in a morning haze,
A fragrant mist cools half-closed eyes.
A sudden shower evokes the blue
Of lawns and landscapes, purple, grey,

Where snow is apple blossom and
Its petals hasten in the breeze.
Here noble ladies in green silk
Sit upright as their horses graze.'

Kiki Triumphs Over the Opposition

At four o'clock each afternoon
Trapeze artistes with aeroplane
Leapt from a jutting balcony
Then, swinging from the Eiffel Tower,

Rendered Piaf. But still,
When Kiki reached the final verse
Of 'Love Songs' of Desnos, the crowd
Crowned her the Queen of Montparnasse.

A Long Sitting

Dawn rose above a fringe of trees,
Only to be waylaid by clouds.
A cypress tree seemed prominent,
Too forthright for the uncertain light.

Before a wine glass pyramid,
When Desnos ordered *soupe du jour*,
The sleepy waiter dropped his towel,
Then, rising, sadly said, '*Which jour?*'

Florence Gould's First Wedding Night

The moon rose with a knowing look.
The marvellous stood on every side,
Like stage sets stacked against the stage.
They tipped the sexton. He allowed

The couple on their wedding night
Alone in Chartres' sapphire groves
To see that blue admit the moon
Like champagne poured through crystal sieves.

The Dependent Moon

The moon itself gives light enough
To make the night sky round it blue,
And yet its beams must still reproach
A world of narrative in which

It plays no part. Its calm belies
Dependence. For, not only does
It need the sun to shine at all,
It waits also the lovers' gaze.

Reticence

Two models sit beside the sea,
Conversing, sifting sand through hands
Which gesture as they laugh and sigh.
They sift the Past and let it fall,

While Pascin smokes and sketches them.
They watch the waves which, lying back
Like them, in lowered tones, confide.
They have no need to leave their mark.

A Surfeit of Kiki's Admirers

'That famous blouse!' the florist said.
'How does she make it fall, from first
One shoulder then the other, then
Show glimpses of a dazzling breast?

I've only one complaint. Since she
Was crowned the Queen of Montparnasse,
My shop has been besieged. By nine,
There's not one red rose in the place.'

The Picnic Party Returns After One Week

Pascin was wading in the stream:
'While other stones have lain unmoved
Here for a thousand years, this one
I recognise. It is the stone

Derain threw here a week ago
Across the spillway's pleated shawl;
And here in the vortex is the plank
Still circling where we saw it fall.'

Curious Memories of the Song of Roland

The waiter spreads a fresh white cloth
Where Oliver and Roland wait.
'We'll have the *soupe du jour, garçon.*'
'That is both brave and wise, my lords.'

Then Roland, acting on a dare,
Stands up and plays a loud glissade,
And history stirs like froth on waves
Or shadows on the palisade.

A Persistent Intrusion

Some startled patrons look askance
As Roland puts the trumpet down.
But then the pianist resumes
And Oliver confides at once,

'The waitress is my sister Aude.
I'll introduce you to her when
She brings our vol-au-vent.' At that,
A hundred starlings rise and turn.

Lee Miller Takes Coffee

A metonym for all the world,
For all the world like life itself,
She sits each morning at the Dôme,
Beneath the birch trees' silver maze.

Preserver of genetic codes,
She sips a coffee. Those who gaze
Are dazzled by the Rayogram
Developing before their eyes.

A Last Vestige of the Fictive Past

At breakfast in her silk chemise
Aude whispered in her brother's ear;
So Oliver ran to the Rotonde
Where camphor trees were turning red:

'Is Roland here? He's wanted now
To play the trumpet in our blues…
Well, if you see him, tell him Aude
Is waiting in her dancing shoes.'

A Duel

'The duel,' explained Apollinaire,
'Was fought for "honour", but, in fact,
Gottlieb espouses Munch, Van Gogh,
While Kisling leans towards Derain.

One second had his best suit slashed.
The swords at length gave way to wine.
Then Kisling proudly named his wound
"Poland partitioned yet again."'

Kisling Expresses Pleasure in His Work

Leaning against a sloping wall
The sun appeared equivocal
About the time of day. A tree
Cast several shadows. Kisling smiled.

'They say that on propitious days
The sundial falls behind the clock;
And when my work is prospering,
Such days must surely bring me luck.'

Kisling and His Models at the Beach

A steam tram took them to the coast.
There on the winter quilted sand
They spread their offerings: Brie, red wine,
A scattering of fruit; and then,

Their own white tableaux in the sun.
Then in that sun's confiding rays
Sea nymphs approached the shore. Were they
Indifferent or intent on praise?

Stardust

The crowd sought wisdom at the Dôme.
Max Jacob said, 'I like to think,
Of Thor or Jupiter in the sky
Grown tired of thunderbolts at last

And throwing down instead on us
A thousand moments like a cloud
Of stardust over Montparnasse,
Some touching Kiki in her bed.'

Origins of the Famous Name

Then Kiki said, 'You must have heard
How our celebrity got his name.
A trumpet broke the firmament
Birds whirled. The signs were favourable

And when the midwife clapped her hands
As if she sensed his future fame
And called out loudly, "It's a man!"
Man Ray drew breath and had his name.'

Kiki and Man Celebrate the Millennia

On holiday one white-waved day,
They watched a man employed to climb
A bristle-cone where birds threw down
Cones on the heads of passers-by.

While parrots disapproved, he climbed
That tree (whose weather rings enshrine
Millennia of sunlit days),
To throw cones safely to the lawn.

Modigliani is Surprisingly Chastened

This sensual young man went south
And visited the frail Renoir,
Who said, 'Paint with the joy of love.
Caress your paintings as I do!

I spend a week or two, at least,
Caressing the backsides of my nudes.'
Modigliani blushed and paused:
'Monsieur! I do not like backsides.'

Intricacies of Spring

The tables still were wet with dew.
The waiter brought a towel. The air
Had news of blossom. Everything
Seemed flecked and speckled, clothed in leaf.

Geometry was cloaked in buds.
Kiki's loose blouse fell pleasantly.
'Look!' Pascin said. 'Who could accept
The Cubists' lean reality?'

Cabbage Palms at Dusk

Kiki and Man were strolling down
An avenue of palms, whose arms,
Like cormorant wings spread out to dry,
And bright tobacco-coloured bracts

Almost locked out a lurid sky.
Their shadows criss-crossed Kiki's own:
A time for photographs, while still
The earth turned slowly from the sun.

Jeanne Hébuterne

Three photographs of Jeanne survive.
She dreams. She does not smile, but stares
As if contending with a world
Already distant long ago.

Some friends found them a studio
And had a stove installed. She smiled:
Modi had painted all the walls
Deep orange, ochre, peach-tinged gold.

At the Brink

In the valley, winter wind
Has blown away the sultry air
And made the shoals of rock shine out,
Like confidences in a glass.

This atmosphere now takes the form
Of one who perilously leans:
Outside the guard rail, near the Leap –
Brash Kiki eating madeleines.

The Fountain Speaks in Berkeleyan Terms

The fountain floating at its plume,
Each profile rising to dissolve
In others, calls, 'Look! Look at me!
Not yet! Not yet! Not yet! Yet now!

We'll stay a moment if you'll watch,
And photographs would help today!
Without your flattering gaze we fall –
We need you here! Don't turn away.'

Overtures and Indifference

Kiki and Man wandered before
The fountain and the poplar tree
Which sang in unison, 'We may
Not be quite as we seem. But yes,

We'd like to mean much more to you.
So, watch us swaying like the reeds…'
But, in the fig trees' busy shade,
No such attention from the birds.

Avant-garde

Encouraged to be modernist,
In Sonia's gowns the women pressed
Round Foujita for photographs.
'A great success at parties,' now

He led the craze for hand-spun skirts,
Greek sandals and the simple life.
Next, tiring of that Spartan role
He flourished Cubism like a scarf.

The Domestic Life

Man Ray and Kiki went to call
On friends returned from holidays.
A cat was sleeping at the door.
'We thought you might be still away.'

'We didn't go. We planned it all;
We left, were on the road, the boat
Was idling at the pier. But then
We felt too sad without our cat.'

The Abandoned Holiday

'Pull up a chair. No. That one's his.
He's very quiet, don't you think?
Perhaps he thinks we still might go
Again, and leave him out alone.

The ferry drifted at the pier
The moment passed, the sea was now
Remote and calm. We came back home.
It was a case of *faute de miaou*.'

Preparing to Paint

The springs welled up in open ground.
The pin-oaks held their darkened leaves,
And palms and tree-ferns kept their heads
Where, shimmering in the frozen pool,

They cast their shadows further off.
This could be just the place to paint –
The light was good. But first things first –
Pascin relit his cigarette.

Schubert's Music Likened to Kiki's Dressmaking

Whole sequences at will could be
Related unexpectedly:
Like two long dresses Man Ray bought
For Kiki – Schiaparelli gowns

Which Kiki one bright afternoon
With 'Dinah' on the gramophone,
Unhesitating cut in halves
And, interchanging, joined again.

Man Ray Invokes Courbet

'Where dark accretions reach the crest,
But here and there a rock face gleams
And, far below these seeping walls,
Sunlight prescribes the ideal field,

We're sitting on the railing when
A sandal falls from Kiki's heel.
We watch it fall until a point
Of darkness on the darkening shale.'

Market Currency

The tuberose-entangled wall
Gave pleasant aspects of the stair
And street fair in the boulevard,
Which smelt of lions, waffles, milk,

Acetylene and sauerkraut.
Here in a sudden shower Fernande
Gave all Foujita's sketches for
A long umbrella like a wand.

Kiki's Renowned Generosity

One morning Kiki near the Dôme,
With friends, saw suddenly appear
Some tourists with their Baedeker.
'They look so desolate,' she cried.

'What can we do for these poor folk?'
And then she smiled. 'I know,' she said,
'What kindness bids me do.' She bent,
And threw her skirts above her head.

Compromises

The view's half-hidden by new leaves.
The lawns are dandelion. Weed flags
Bend in the rain. Clouds hide the sun.
Some daisies, like an afterthought,

Spread randomly. The river bends
To part the woods. The sky's a haze.
Pascin is unsure where to start,
Outdone by so much compromise.

War and Peace

Pascin and Hermine, dragging out
Old trunks of papers locked away
During the war, had carried one
Into the courtyard's snow-bright light.

A drawing from the sombre past
Spilled into post-war, dappled air –
Of Lucy from the sunlit past,
Her peaceful gaze his conqueror.

A Passion

Brancusi lured his neighbour's fowl
As dinner for his guests. He played
Duets with Satie, then described
His prowess on the golf course. 'But,'

Cried Satie, 'Golf is English. Not
A game a sane Roumanian plays.'
Brancusi drove the ball. It flew.
It struck the wall. It broke a vase.

To Lucy

In adolescence Per Krogh knew
That strong desire for nothingness,
To fill the day with emptiness,
To let time pass as through a sieve.

To Pascin and Hermine he said,
'I'm happy now,' and raised his glass.
'In love, one gives away one's self.
Living? Our loves do that for us.'

Winter Dreams

While Aude and Roland danced all night
In overcoats, in ghosting air,
Near where the river shouldered ice,
And soon the mill wheel froze to rest,

Kiki was sleeping with a smile
And little else, dreaming again
Of battlements and charming snow,
Beneath her satin eiderdown.

Kiki Meets Treize

'One day I saw, outside the Dôme,
A girl whose hat was like my own,
Which seemed no more than an excuse
For large bouquets of cherries. So

I followed her inside. We danced.
The hat was on the barman's head.
He laughed and said, "Don't wake Desnos,
He picnics with the festive dead."'

Desnos Meets Treize

Desnos woke from a waking dream
And found himself in love. 'What is
This thing called love?' he asked anew
As these two danced the day away.

The barman wearing Kiki's hat
Stood laughing. Near him, Kiki with
One who seemed – Indescribable!
'Keats was right. Beauty is Truth.'

An Effusion

Lucy is reading from a book
By some young protégé. She chants,
'…The white which gathers round events
Like white foam ruffling round the prow…'

'Come off it, Lucy,' someone cries.
'You've had too much.' 'Not so,' she says.
'It's true. That is the waterfall
Which plunges only as we gaze.'

Clouds

Man Ray saw film developing
Like underwater willow leaves
Whose silver ferns of flocculate
Appear first round the emerging forms,

A mesh of white in tangled wands,
A sudden flash of sky, now caught:
Then someone opened the darkroom door
Flooding the amber world with light.

A Parabola Near Courbet's Ornans

The sandstone cliff which faced the falls
Across the plunging gorge, the wind
Had hollowed to a shallow cave.
And, at the focus of this curve,

The sound of falling water grew
And gathered to a deafening roar.
Kiki and Treize stood marvelling
Until their laughter broke the air.

At the Coast

A summer's day with single cloud,
Which, from first light, presided at
The cobalt sea and azure sky,
Drew Treize and Kiki out of doors.

And then, as if they knew Desnos
Quested in dreams at La Coupole,
They walked beside but did not dive
Into the sea's unwaking swell.

A Little-known Fact

The day Modigliani died
Or, rather, on the following night
And yet before Jeanne Hébuterne
Leapt from the room and out of time,

His cat also leapt to its death.
This sad and inexplicable fact
Is well attested and reproves
All Histories for its neglect.

Homages to Manet

Pine needles fell like tuning-forks
In spirals to the forest lawn.
Only black Coco, Pascin's cat,
Was listening to their ringing tone.

The rest of us lay on the grass
In homage to the *Déjeuner*.
Then Kiki cried, seizing the cat,
'I'll be Olympia for the day.'

Natalie Barney at Her Temple à L'Amitié

Her salon, it was once remarked,
Was like a field of flowering grass
With unstrung lutes and oddities
Disposed on chairs, dark peppermint creams,

'Damp sandwiches like handkerchiefs'
On gold plates, served by this Amazon,
Who 'got a lot from life, perhaps
More than was in it. Thus she shone.'

Autobiography of Natalie Barney

'My first erotic stirrings came
When, as a child I had the task
Of massaging the upstretched arms
Of models in a lengthy pose.

For men have skin, but women flesh,
A flesh which takes and gives back light;
In me a mute Pygmalion toiled,
Who daily grew more passionate.'

Café Table Talk Concerning the New Physics

'They do say all's uncertain now;
Suppose that cup's an atom and
That glass another, and I glance
From that salt cellar down that ray,

The light, you see, by gravity
Is bent to that pot of English tea.
So that our gaze moves in a curve
Suggesting Kiki's *déshabillé*.'

A 360° View

Max Jacob dancing on the bar
Saw, standing up to take his turn
One he might like to irritate.
Apollinaire now read aloud.

And from his vantage on the bar,
As ancient trees command the plain,
Max listened gravely. Then he said,
'Alas! Too Symbolist again.'

At the Temple

While tea and cakes and sandwiches,
With gin 'for the Americans'
Accompanied a Sapphic play,
And Natalie as shepherdess

Presided in the ivy gloom,
Next, listeners languished in the dark,
As several actors at full tilt
Severely rendered 'La Jeune Parque'.

Meanwhile, Outside the Temple

The author of 'La Jeune Parque'
Arrived quite late one afternoon.
The cakes and tea were almost gone.
Outside the palisade he heard

The cries of actors in full flight.
'I thought I heard outside the gate
The sound of someone being killed,
But it was only my Young Fate.'

Indulgences

In Rumpelmayer's, Natalie
Indulged in *mousse au chocolat*,
And savoured her new freedom since
Despatching Dolly Wilde by train.

But suddenly, framed in the door,
Stood Dolly, tears darkening her dress!
At length the lovers, reconciled,
Wept happily into the mousse.

Dolly's Return

'Such tears! The fact that you exist,
Kept washing over me in waves,
And in their foam, such memories!
The train kept climbing, and the south,

Retreating in a widening arc,
Without you seemed remote, austere.
I left the train, and crossed the line,
And caught the next train back, my dear.'

Natalie Barney and Dolly Wilde Walk Together

The gaps between the silver birch
Grew wider as they walked. Below,
Against the slate dark river's gleam
The barges slowly slipped from view.

The pleasures of reunion bloom
Mysteriously, and soon must fade.
Before they'd reached the Temple gate
Thoughts of new loves imposed their shade.

Sylvia Beach and Adrienne Monnier Meet

As in a poster by Lepape
This Sylvia turned to read the air
Which spring wrote in the avenue
And light had published in the trees,

Her hand poised at the bookshop door;
The breeze then plucked her wide straw hat,
And Adrienne, in peasant skirt,
Pursued it down the book-lined street.

Derain From His Great Height

Where firs of aniseed increase
Between the ancient jetty boards,
Derain, in search of subjects, finds
A ferry lying on its side,

Awash, its stateroom quite submerged.
He's curious, then pontificates.
'Painting,' he says, 'refloats the self
From the Present's great submerging weights.'

Ballet Mécanique For Player Piano

At Pleyel's rooms, the audience
Grew restive at the first wide chords,
And soon were more cacophonous
Than Antheil's music. Someone screamed.

Asked how he could endure such scorn
Benoist-Méchin smiled. 'Don't forget
It's not a piano. I pedal fast
And feel I'm escaping them on foot.'

L'Amour Fou

That love which distances the past
Propelled Desnos: 'The day we met,
The sea divided, or, let's say,
The Styx was floodlit, spring sprang up,

Luxe, Calme et Volupté occurred,
Repeated all along its shores.
Yvonne George drove a path between
My life and all that ever was.'

A Garden Stage

Just as 'the classical guitar
Not softly sounds but from afar,'
So the blackbird. Others shrill
From centre stage. But blackbirds bring

Glissandi, melismatic trills
And spacious silences, and there,
As breezes gather through the leaves,
They draw back curtains on the air.

Lee Miller Saved

When absent-mindedly she stepped
Into the path of moving cars
And Condé Nast, *Vogue* publisher,
Had plucked her back, she stood, as if

Precipitating silver cells,
Resplendent, radiant, still as calm
As soon she would appear in *Vogue*
With blossom trailing from her arm.

Lee Miller's Rescuer Sees Her Future Radiance

Plucked from the path of progress, brought
In safety to the kerb, she stood
Approaching on a fluted shell,
Propelled by clamorous zephyrs' breaths.

At once, he saw her face in *Vogue*:
Long languid eyes and dazzling neck,
The beauty of her curling lips,
That crucial absence all men seek.

Alternative Catalogue of Delights

Kisling awoke among the limbs
Of several deep in sleep. He saw
A bloom of light still tentative
On cup and bowl and wrist and thigh

And then on curves less often praised:
Veins in the foot, a forearm's hinge,
The sternum pale between the breasts,
An elbow's grace, the combed hair's fringe.

Waking at La Coupole, Desnos is Confronted

'You mean you don't know Zadkine, or
Brancusi's white *Young Girl*? It is
The most delicious, beautiful,
Most female derrière in the world.'

She drank another brandy, smiled
And lit another rank Gauloise.
And, all the while, she never once
Averted those grey, searching eyes.

Desnos on the River with Yvonne George

'The fig trees in a maze of leaves
Imposed horizons of their own,
From which birds flew into a sky
As white as Mallarmé's white page.

And there you have some measure of
The whiteness of her face. The barge
Was knocking idly at the bank.
At dusk she smiled, as if on stage.'

Desnos Engulfed

'The violet evening like a ship
Approached along its long canal.
The trees were cadmium orange. Light
Was pressed like water from a cloth

Between the rows of elms. Somewhere
A piano played "September Song".
At those first notes she gazed at me
And winter hastened into spring.'

Desnos Perplexed

'Before me in the sunlit barge
She lay, so irreducibly
Contained in cells as to confirm
All beauty is an aggregate.

Perhaps what now I loved in her
Were just those qualities which made
Her quite incapable of love.
Beneath the bridge, she smiled in shade.'

Desnos Succumbs

'The carmine evening slowly fell
Like a ladder lowered to the stage.
I climbed down to the river bank
And stood below the Notre Dame

Just at that point where, I was told,
Some medieval roué fell.
I leaned against the yellow stone
And crumpled under love's vast spell.'

Desnos' Long Day

'And on that last predestined day,
We were to meet outside the Dôme.
I waited. First an open rose
Came floating by on the canal.

The wind arrived, with pollen, blown
From the hinterland. Stars came out.
Then, slowly, down the steps, she came.
As if she lived only by night.'

Pascin Chances on a Subject

The distant ziggurat, the tree
Which slants across the picture plane,
The palm obscurely vertical,
The cliffs above the running stream

All yield the palm with much acclaim
To bathers bending at the ford.
Against the landscape's dappled page
Their whiteness shimmers like a sword.

In Brancusi's White Studio

A white magnolia shone. A dog
As white as settled snow lay down.
The walls washed white provided no
Distraction to the soaring bird.

Even his hair and beard were white.
Then someone brought a troubling sight:
Snapdragons challenging the room,
Complex in form, flesh pink, noon bright.

Far Away, Desnos Thinks of Yvonne George

Leaning over the fence to stroke
The mare pressed hotly to his hand,
He felt her belly and flank's weight
Remote yet overwhelmingly

Immediate and sentient.
He thought of the actress on the stage,
Unknowable and yet more real
Than all his life, that wind-turned page.

A Pastoral Far from the Theatre

The orange trees' dark green recedes.
Desnos is calm as if asleep.
Two horses nuzzle near a fence,
Dark chestnut in a clover field,

An arching bridge with flanking tails.
Behind them where each poplar shades
The river in a pencil line,
The sun is working, lifting clouds.

Art and Life

The painter of the *Demoiselles*,
Proponent of the tribal mask
And drastic angularity,
In summer liked the seaweed beach,

And ambling with his many friends.
He waits until they pause and bend
To look at shells or coloured sand,
Then photographs them from behind.

Ninety-one Paintings by Pascin and Kisling

While war raged on across the straits,
The good ship *Montparnasse* drove on
Into the icy northern swell
With Halvorsen strapped at the helm,

Avoiding German submarines.
At length he telegraphed the news:
The exhibition had arrived;
All paintings safe on Norway's shores.

The Uses of Poetry

On Tuesdays at the Closerie
Paul Fort declaimed while others drank.
The Symbolists, Apollinaire,
Were published in his *Vers et Prose*,

The bulk of which were never sold
But served as chairs in every room.
Some copies were despatched by post
Wheeled slowly there by baby's pram.

A Happy Day in Verse and Prose

When Marinetti lent his bright
Bugatti to the lucky pair,
She, 'absolutely beautiful',
He, signed-up Futurist and groom,

Gino and Jeanne (née Fort), drove to
The Café Voltaire, showered with rice.
The money for the autumn run
Of *Vers et Prose* paid for the place.

A Wedding Present

Someone had given bride and groom
A Winged Victory of Samothrace
In plaster. This took pride of place.
Max Jacob, on a table, danced

And then, to everyone's surprise,
Cried out, 'This *Victory*, as you know,
To all true Futurists, is Past',
And smashed it with a joyful blow.

Bronia After the Death of Radiguet

'Never have I felt, before,
Such generous susurrations, such
Sweet waves of recompense for all
The sorrows of the world. The sea

Flows darkly underneath the prow.
Oncoming surges spray apart
But never break across the deck
As this his absence breaks my heart.'

Bronia at Late Afternoon

The sun lay down between the waves,
The shadow of the sail turned pale
Then vanished from the deck. The swell
Rose up then disappeared below

The calm accommodating prow.
The deck was dry, its boards still warm.
'He cast no shadows,' Bronia said.
'This was the secret of his charm.'

Bronia and Radiguet Wading Among Similes

At dawn they walked along the pier.
The sea was like the scales of fish
Seen swimming in the sea. Still dark,
A trawler floated in the tide.

Then, swimming with a glistening tail,
The sun contended with low cloud
Like cormorants who dip and dive,
Emerging somewhere else through weed.

Brief Glimpse of Reality at the Rotonde

'We back up to the Present, just
As horses back into a stall,
And soon we'll feel that ocean spray,
That actual aura of events –

As scientists will one day know
What happened when the world began…'
Soon after this brave utterance
Desnos was sleeping once again.

A Wedding

At Kisling's wedding to Renée
The party lasted three loud days,
Took in the brothels of Saint Germain
And caviar and borrowed wine.

Modi appeared as Caesar's ghost.
(Renée cried out, 'My bridal sheets!')
At dawn the naked groom was found
Curled up on canvases with cats.

Pronouncements

At Breton's house on Rue Fontaine
The nights were spent in argument
On love and sex and destiny,
L'amour courtois and *l'amour fou*,

Until Kiki at length cried, 'Well!
You men are full of words! And yet
Not one of you poor creatures knows
To love is to forget all that.'

Desnos Offers a Compliment

'So, Breton's job with Gallimard,
Is reading Proust aloud to Proust.
An enviable task, you might suppose,
To catalogue that plane tree's leaves,

Yet I would vastly rather sit
Here in these beech leaves' light, with you,
And turn the pages of your gaze,
With not a written word in view.'

Leaving the Dôme

Pascin stepped out into the street
Into the dazzling heart of light,
The day's dividing calyx. There,
He felt the strange delight and fear

Of one who walks into a square
Beset by leaves, well known, yet vague
Which in their shade seems strangely new.
He was in love with Lucy Krohg!

Eternal Triangle

Per Krohg is standing by the pool,
Half hidden in the pine tree's shade.
A radio plays 'These Foolish Things'
While Lucy suns herself and waits.

Pascin approaches. Then Lucy sees,
As in *Tristan*, that other man
Reflected in the pool. She says,
'We're both pleased you have come, Pascin.'

Arcs

Pascin and Lucy planned to meet
Outside a building of Guimard:
The Jassedé flats – with balconies
Like arching hair combs, windows framed

By sinuous rails. And when they met,
The rain in arabesques curved down:
Their secrecy made all the world
Evasive, wayward, serpentine.

Pascin and Lucy in the South

The valley curtain billowed round
A railway siding long closed down
Where wild narcissus flowers had spread,
A yellow, unselfconscious field,

Which Lucy gathered in her arms.
The landscape bloomed as in a dream.
Where trains uncoupled, now Pascin
Was travelling with a head of steam.

Reunion

To meet a friend upon the crest
Where otherwise the plain extends,
While light bends low, and distance shines,
Appears to stress that curvature

Which on all sides takes worlds away
As ships to harbour come masts first.
Pascin and Krohg again embrace
And Lucy smiles, by each caressed.

Admiration Divided

Kisling is painting, *en plein air*,
Bronia With Polyanthus Flowers,
And sees their confluence of sighs.
'It comes to this. Whose face is more

Outgoing, generous and grave?
The flowers with their billowing hues?
Or Bronia choosing whitewashed light?
What sentience in both! What eyes!'

Pascin Improvises

'A figured gown with stiff gold lace,
A mantle hemmed by yellow silk,
Through which a thistle pattern ran:
Aeneas' gift to Dido! So

My gift to Lucy for the ball!
It came to me quite late last night.
I'm at my best at night. But then,
I couldn't find a cigarette.'

Dufy

Fearing his own facility,
He drew left-handed. Doctor Viard
Remembered seeing him at work
Each hand engaged on different themes.

A turning-point came with Matisse.
Quite suddenly Impressionism
Seemed less impressive. In its place
A wash of cobalt filled the chasm.

Josephine Takes Chiquita for a Walk

Pascin put down a bowl of milk
Beside the tables at the Dôme,
Beneath a cloudless fimbriate sky.
'A pantheress with gilded claws'

Who wore a snake coiled round her neck
(To separate the men and boys),
And led a leopard on a leash,
Stopped while it lapped with purring noise.

Maurice Denis Questioned

'Remember that, before it is
A woman's face or vase of blooms,
A painting is essentially
A surface of assembled tones…'

His friends gazed at the sea and sky.
'But all we see are surfaces,
Each one a maze of shades and tones.
So, what is new in all of this?'

Enter Lee. Exit Kiki

'Man Ray said, "What's your name?" I said,
"Lee Miller. You must call me Lee.
I've come to be your student." He
Said, "Lee, I don't have students. And

I'm leaving now for Biarritz."
And I said, "So am I." Somewhere
Across the bar blazed Kiki's gaze,
A white gazelle pawing the air.'

Lee Miller Invents Solarisation

When, in the darkroom in the dark,
Lee felt some creature scuttle by
Across her foot, she screamed and, lurching,
Turned on the light, exposing there

The rolls of film developing,
All floating in their secret bath.
Man held them to the light. He smiled:
She'd added haloes like a breath.

Everyone For Tennis

The Countess Pecci-Blunt decreed
That everyone should dress in white.
Lee bought a gown like summer snow,
But Man insisted he and she

Should go as tennis players. So,
While he projected, from above,
Old screen romances on their heads
She volleyed every beam to love.

Still at the White Ball of the Pecci-Blunts

The dancers circled, all in white.
Man Ray projected, from above,
Old Méliès pictures onto them;
(Faces and titles could be read).

Lee Miller was assisting him,
In white also, white as a dove.
He felt distracted, ill at ease
To find himself falling in love.

Man Ray's Famous Painting

The lips that span the cirrus sky
Above the twin observatory
Were Kiki's rosebud mouth at first
Imprinted on the artist's shirt.

The canvas hung above his bed
Long after Kiki said farewell
And passed, like a vision on the stairs,
Lee Miller's enigmatic smile.

Caresse Crosby Contemplates the Great Men

'Just after Harry had the sun
Tattooed across his back, he walked
To Luxor in the dusk and found
Rimbaud carved deeply in the stone.

And did not Flaubert find, one dawn,
High on the Giza pyramid,
A business card with fateful name?
Just think! My favourite, famous Dead.'

A Landscape by Kisling

The engine climbs the slate incline.
The calcite bright embankments shine.
Against them, like the letter 'N'
Repeated where white smoke has been,

The double power poles in line
Appear to spell a monotone.
A cypress tree leans like a hand
While from the tunnel steams the train.

Outrage

When Julien Lévy would not be
Her lover, there and then, one bright,
Warm sunlit morning, Kiki said
To Treize, her friend, 'I told him straight,

"*Vous n'êtes pas un homme mais un hommelette.*"
The nerve! I posed for him. The bore
Expected me to pose again.
I mean, what does he take me for?'

Satie and Disappointing Weather

The pearl-grey sky, like fingernails
By Poiret, glistened and diffused
The light above the brickworks wall.
The barman said, 'It looks like rain,

So, soon we'll see Saint Erik here.'
Just then the sun broke through the veil
And from the door, umbrella raised,
A voice complained, 'Busy old fool!'

Chanel vs Poiret

One evening in the theatre's glow
As Monsieur Jourdain studied 'prose',
Then, turbanned like the Great Turk, danced,
Chanel looked round the audience

And saw a room of women dressed
Elaborately as those on stage.
She cried, 'This cannot last! I'll dress
Them in a simple black corsage.'

Sensuality

That summer when the heatwave came
The Sphinx grew famous overnight.
It was the first house to install
Le Airconditioning. Then the call,

'*Tu viens?*' would bring a knowing smile.
'Upstairs with you? Sure. OK. Please!'
For then, up there, it was delight
To feel that cool, delicious breeze.

Stravinsky and Chanel: an Elegant Encounter

Coco undressed. The 'little black',
Le luxe dans la simplicité,
Announcing worlds it had concealed,
Fell draped at Igor's feet. He smiled,

Folding his trousers in their pleats:
'I recommend my new régime
Of raw potatoes thinly sliced
In oil, with just a touch of thyme.'

Stravinsky Breaks His Diet

'*Etonne-moi*' now was in the air;
Even the sun obliged. All day,
The light was startling at the Dôme.
Stravinsky, in this spirit, took

A fellow diner's cutlet. 'This,'
He raised his fork and gravely said,
'Will presently astonish all
The raw potatoes I have had.'

Youki's Twenty-first Birthday

Waking, she stepped aboard the day
As to a running-board, that car
About to glide towards delight.
Foujita bought for her a large

Yellow Ballot (with Basque chauffeur)
Which, adding prestige to surprise,
Had on its grille a miniature
Of Rodin's *Man With Broken Nose*.

The Character of Apollinaire

He loved all fruit. And in his suit
He sought out old engraving shops.
He hated working at a table.
The fruits he loved were spheres which hold

An embarrassment of juices. He
Assumed so many characters,
Even the bank asked him to give
Eleven different signatures.

Un Coup de Dés

Two lovers shared Lee Miller's bed
So amicably that when she left
To sail aboard the *Comte de Grasse*,
They tossed a coin to see which one

Should see her off. The loser flew
His biplane low above the deck,
Scattering yellow roses… Then
A plane-crash crowned his losing streak.

Marie Laurencin's Portraits of Women

One day when light rain fell all day
Marie served tea to everyone,
With cakes, on an embroidered cloth
(Apollinaire's face stitched in black).

She was accompanied by her cat
Who disapproved of cakes, and who,
Marie explained, had posed for all
The faces in her portraits too.

Apollinaire In Love

'Marie has come to visit me
And brought a skipping rope and skipped
Through all the garden. As you know
My rooms are on the second floor –

She skipped downstairs! And at the gate,
She gave what's called a vinegar turn –
The rope is spun three times. This means
"Goodbye for now. I'll see you soon."'

The Approaching Influenza Epidemic

Standing on their anchored barge,
His daughter with a magazine,
Paul Poiret gravely said, 'Rosine,
Once, women were architectural,

And splendid, like the prow of ships.
Now they resemble in their black,
Some underfed telephonists…'
Rosine smiled sadly, strangely, back.

Passage of Afternoon

At noon, deep shadow spread, like clothes
Shed round the feet of languid trees.
Pascin and Lucy found this shade
And lay where tassels spiralled down.

As dusk approached, Lucy returned
To find a handkerchief mislaid;
And light seemed brighter where they'd lain
Than anywhere above the glade.

Pretentiousness at La Coupole

'The world's an upturned pyramid
Of empty glasses. Right? The light
Goes through the lot. Somewhere out there,
Our generation works to keep

That teetering stable. All the while,
A sky of glasses glitters where
A palm frond leans a genial arm
Along the splashed horizon's bar.'

Ink Drawing With Wash

The nesting swallows fly within
An air of least resistance, close
Above the surface of the lake,
And far below the lowering clouds

Whose pillars rise like cypress trees.
Soon it will rain. And, still, Pascin
Sketches the scene until large drops
Create an innovative stain.

Apollinaire: a Brief Biography

Born Kostrowitzky, soon by friends
Called Cointreauwhiskey; Poem shaped
Like a cube; Theft of the *Mona Lisa*;
Poem shaped like the Eiffel Tower;

Cubism in the Foreign Legion;
Head bandaged at the Café de Flore;
Lascivious sorrows; Marie! Marie!
Women shaped like the Eiffel Tower.

Desnos and the Coup de Foudre

Outside the Coupole, 'Let Stendhal
Describe the onset of our love:
"They throw a leafless, winter branch
Into the abandoned mine. And soon

Each twig is thick with diamond salt…
Love is a crystallising snow."
So. In my cavernous heart I bear
A heavy, bright, encrusted bough.'

Approval

As Bronia danced and René Clair
Asked her to marry, then and there,
And Kiki had roses in her hair,
And Pascin sketched with coffee grounds,

And Flossie Martin sang above
The piano in the crowded bar,
A cat uncurled in someone's arms,
And smiling assent, began to purr.

Zadkine Praises the Crenellations of the Potato

'Our enemy is Euclid. Look!
Geometry should not exist.
Straight lines should curve and bend and tangle.
Even Constantin's deceived

By smoothness as simplicity –
His Bird's a mere cigar – while I
Dislike even the full moon,
That sterile circle in the sky.'

Octave Mirbeau's Hotel Encounter

'Let me confide. This afternoon
I chanced on someone in my room:
Raised arms, a torso white as snow
A froth of lace caught in fair hair.

I closed the door. She cried, "Monsieur,
Monsieur!" The mirror made her shine.
The bed was spread with dresses, gloves.
"Monsieur!" she said, more faintly then.'

After That Encounter

'I genuinely mistook the room
I thought such things never occurred…'
Sitting at dinner, he mused and smiled.
And then he blushed. Into the room

A couple – she most elegant,
And he much older, stout, austere –
Approached his table. She blushed too,
Contriving that they sit elsewhere.

Qualified Contentment

The kapok trees rained down a floss
Of flocculating light. the sun
Trailed spiders' webs on everyone.
Equality, Fraternity

Touched everyone around the Dôme,
As if some stranger stood champagne.
Satie was happy but for this:
He would have liked a little rain.

Conversations at the Dingo

'Asked for my passport, I just say,
"My name is Edna St Vincent Millay."
It never fails.' 'Brancusi struck
The ball. It bounded from the wall

And broke a vase. He liked it that
The ball was white.' 'That nightdress, yes!
I spent that summer looking for
A night deserving of that dress.'

Kisling in Need of Sleep

And facing every way at once
Her body seemed to fill the room
With tropic and intemperate zones.
She held the pose. His eyes swam.

He felt himself adrift, afloat,
Stretched out along a compass beam
In a world in which magnetic north
Existed only in a dream.

A Landscape Painter Visits Brancusi

Looking at distance and biting off
Much more than he could chew, he knew
The whole was too – unmanageable…
And yet he found some ease, at dusk,

When, in his whitewashed studio,
Brancusi calmly broke up all
He'd made that day, then fed his dogs
Their milk and lettuce in a bowl.

A Serviette by Desnos

A scrap of paper spiralling
Into the clouds about to break
Contains perhaps the only use
Of a certain adjective linked with

A certain noun. No one will know:
For dark dissolves to shredded silk
And flooded chairs are left in haste.
Later, the light returns, like milk.

Overheard at the Dingo

'I've just been watching Vallotton.
He starts a painting at the top –
The left hand corner generally –
And works his way down to the right.

Now, what does that remind me of?
The sort of day I'd like to have
Which traces out a single path,
A day which fits me like a glove.'

Dufy at Nice

'An unexpected fall of snow
At carnival had turned the palms
To waiters' arms raised high, with trays
Of shining sorbets, glistening glaces.

These changes may exemplify
Those necessary to our art
Whereby things thought immutable
Must step aside to free the heart.'

Chez Kisling: *Luxe, Calme et Volupté*

Verlaine, by London Sundays charmed,
And Prévert, in whose poetry
'*Jeunes filles*' are '*belles*' and often '*nues*',
Would have approved this chaste tableau:

Steamed milk and coffee, croissants shared,
A peignoir, quilt, a silver tray,
Newspapers on the sunlit bed,
Languorous arms in disarray.

Sunday

Bronia is standing at the sill,
She leans to see the square below.
The distant bandstand entertains
The Sunday lawns. Then, sudden rain

As suddenly has passed. And next,
Bowing and scraping, cap in hand,
The sun appears through shreds of cloud,
Conciliatory, cheering the band.

More Painters' Talk

'We see light first, and only then
Does colour separate and so
Declare itself. And in that pause
All the affective world draws breath,

Then breaks like waves across our bows.'
The barman frowned. 'I'm ill at ease.
I doubt if I can mix your drinks
The way you mix those metaphors.'

Kisling Waxes Eloquent

'Events, of course, are Pointillist,
But when the thing's falsely applied
To stasis (and the eye can move
And find this flux no flux at all),

That's when our problems start. But look!
Don't look too hard at anything.
Colour already divides the world.
Just try to see things happening.'

And Scarcely Knows When to Stop

'Don't look too hard at anything.
The eye's not meant to break a stone,
And when the model rests and talks,
She well may be most visible.

The whole is more or less the sum
Of less than all its parts. The rest
Is always with us. Fill your glass.
Press on once more without the Past.'

A Modernist Manifesto

Apollinaire with bandaged head
Expatiated at the Dôme.
'You say, my friend, there's nothing new
Under the sun. I can't agree.

X-rays have seen inside my skull!
And look. Above the figured lane
The clouds are moving for a storm
In forms no one has ever seen!'

Before Rain

The blackbird waited on its bough
Then flew down in a looping bow.
The sun had fallen just below
The awning blind. Apollinaire

Looked backwards as he crossed the lane
Into which turned some vast machine
So large as to seem invisible.
Then first drops touched the Dôme's clear pane.

Kiki Describes a Sunset with Man Ray

'The blue as if of Cythera
Finds clouds arrayed with cadmium.
We float upon the floating pier
While harbour perorations fade

Until dusk falls. Then crickets chirr
Beside the wall, contentedly.
The intermittent wash of waves
Is soon the only white we see.'

Pascin's Palette

The vase of pale ranunculi
Asserts with all due deference
Both critique and an inventory
Of Pascin's palette. They know well

His apricots, his silver greys
Which struggle with vermilions,
His strawberry pinks, silk sepias,
No tone unmixed with other tones.

Gris Is Asked to Perform a Miracle

'The bottle seen as cylinder,
Cezanne's great task. I disagree.
I'd rather the reverse, to make
A bottle from the cylinder.'

'Well,' Kisling said, 'why not start now?
Unless the waiter comes back soon
We'll need that miracle. Meanwhile,
Just turn this water into wine.'

Foujita Paints Anna de Noailles

Because she walked and talked and paced
Incessantly, and would not wait
To look at work in progress, and
Would criticise, 'My dear! My eyes!

They should be lakes! Immense! Profound!'
Foujita painted her in bed,
Still talking. 'If God did exist
He would have told me first… More red!'

Anna de Noailles Continues Breathlessly

'Foujita, my dear, a small surprise:
Go out on to the balcony.
You'll see a sweet white rabbit there
Who lives only on violets. There!

Isn't that terribly Japanese?'
Foujita who had never seen
A rabbit eating violets, said
"Of course. Try not to move. Don't turn."'

Spring Breeze

The willow-wands like kite tails twist;
And to the surface of the field,
Beset by multiplicity,
The distant view adds lichen-green.

Pascin looks on. Today, it seems,
The sun is swayed by every breeze.
Even the snow, blown in the air,
Is petals from the apple trees.

Prévert Recalls an Incident in a Theatre

'An actor friend had stage door keys
And after hours in the wings
He'd pause a long time in that gloom
Then make an entrance. How he trod

The boards – as if already he
Were deluged in bouquets! And all
The while that pause affected me –
Enjambement made visible.'

A Courtyard

Apollinaire in boating hat,
Arrested for the heinous crime
Of stealing the *Mona Lisa*, spent
Six days in gaol, and from his cell

Saw fountain plumes in canon rise,
Which, falling, helped beguile the time:
The fountain and its spray of words
Enacted one vast Calligramme.

The Pleasures of Absence

'The Louvre! Why not come with us?
Make it a party. We'll see where once
The stolen *Mona Lisa* hung.
What mystery! It's all the rage;

The crowds are gathering every day.
They don't want Venuses, or all
That subtle light on poppy fields –
They want this fenced-off piece of wall.'

Prévert Speaks for the Weather

'I want the world to say, "How strange,
That light beside the poplar tree,
The mist still lifting from the sea
An hour behind the rising sun,

That breeze so redolent with the past."
I know I'm quite emotional,
And yet, to clothe the naked world –
Think, if you will, how that must feel.'

Prévert Is Reluctant to Abandon the Subject

'The weather leapt from bed, and said,
"I'll wear my lightest dress today.
Today, I will surpass myself.
My infinite variety

Can start with snow. Next, let the sun
Burn fiercely on the melting plain;
Then a shower which even as it falls
Evaporates in haze again."'

News

All talk was of the hotel maid
Who found the stolen Condé gem
By biting into its hiding place –
An apple in a guest's locked room –

And then, for her dishonesty,
Was sacked. Kiki exclaimed, 'Unfair!
Why! I'd have swallowed it and left
By night train for the Côte d'Azur.'

In the Bar

Pascin put roses in a glass.
'Renoir said, "When I arrange
Some flowers in a vase I find
I paint the side I did not plan."

But let me now elaborate:
Hermine and Lucy! Who can say
In that great serendipity
Which love was planned and which was play?'

Flossie Martin Greets the Tourists

Inside the Dingo, pleasure flowed
Like wine, and wine flowed endlessly.
A blue Rolls Royce pulled up outside
And two rich ladies, draped in furs

Looked through the door. Some coarse remarks
About their character and class
Came floating through the door. One said,
'Come on, Jane. This must be the place.'

Kiki Paints Foujita

'She told me not to move. I sat.
She painted. And she laughed and danced.
She sang some numbers from 'Louise',
Then said that I could look. I found

She'd bitten all my pencils, chewed
The brush stems, lost erasers… There
She stood, delighted. Then I saw
She'd eaten all my Camembert.'

On the Cliffs

A crowd walked out soon after dawn.
The light was faltering, and the day
Had lost direction. Plovers swerved.
Time's arrow vanished in the haze,

As if seized by some nesting bird.
Aude seemed to hear, borne from the Past,
A trumpet practising a phrase
Repeated in the wind-blown mist.

Arabesques

Spring swallows flew in shallow arcs
Across the curving river steps.
Someone was holding forth. 'Take Bach,
Or Notre Dame, or Delacroix...

Their genius is complexity.'
'Then,' Desnos said, 'these swallows show
The greater genius. Their flights
Are complex tropes, supremely so.'

Derain's Model Speaks

'Some painters work from nature. Some
Prefer to let dark memory bloom
Without the subject's teasing flux.
What can you say then of Derain?

He sits the model on his knee
His left hand round her waist, his right
Depicting with the brush the forms
Which touch and sight roundly impart.'

Tunnel Vision

'An escape from Cubism's stifling air'
His racing car, bright powder-blue,
Derain declared, 'more beautiful
Than any work of art,' and drove

At miles a minute to the coast,
The whistling world a windswept glance.
The car outshone the admiring sea,
And palm trees struck an envious stance.

Poiret on the Brink of Bankruptcy

Resplendent, Poiret brought his skills
To dress three barges at the Quay:
Amours, a restaurant of dreams;
Délices, a theatre draped in silk;

And Orgues, a floating gallery
(With fourteen paintings by Dufy).
All this too soon, alas, would be
A valedictory luxury.

Gilliflowers

Rousseau at La Coupole explains,
'With loaded brush I check the tone
Beside the sitter's face. It's best
To paint things as they really are

And count each leaf. I think I'd like
To "finish" paintings by Cezanne –
To indecisive cylinders
Add gilliflowers, leaves and vine.'

At Rousseau's Famous Banquet

Dressed as Delirium, chewing soap,
Cremnitz was frothing at the mouth.
Rousseau himself sat on a throne
With pancake sugar down his clothes;

A dog licked at his trouser leg.
Marie Laurencin in countless ways
Contrived to seem as innocent
And naive as in fact she was.

Ballet Mécanique

A chestnut tree's serrated leaves
Turned golden in the Seine's late light,
Each creased as if unfolded from
An origami bird. Wild flowers

Were lush amongst the chestnut hulls.
Léger walked on, oblivious
To that great flush of cells. He sought
'Steel bolts more beautiful than a rose.'

Anna de Noailles Indisposed

Vuillard, also, had painted her,
Magnificent, upright, in bed.
On this occasion she had said
To her maid, 'Before he comes, remove

That cold cream and thermometer.
For, otherwise, I'll look a fright
With all this detail. For, as you know,
Vuillard paints everything in sight.'

An Incident Related by Vollard

Light clustered round the apples. Then
Exasperated by their smile,
Cezanne had thrown a still life through
The window, where it caught and hung,

For some weeks, in a cherry tree.
But then he asked his son, 'Fetch down
My apples. Bring the longest pole.
I think I'll work on that again.'

Pascin Approaching Midnight

Increasingly I find myself
Advancing eagerly on the next
Of all our lives. It waits, a mere
Blue dive away, into the pool

Below our craning tower. Each day
That blue of lapis, or Capri,
Seems sweeter, more voluptuous.
I take that breath. It beckons me.

The Inviolate Bed

The coverlet was white, and glowed,
Immaculate, like untouched snow,
Or light caught in a golden elm.
No one could lean or touch or sit

Or place a hat upon its field.
'If you would love Apollinaire,'
His mistress said once to her friend,
'Expect to make love in a chair.'

Last Days

Pascin and Lucy drifted. Once
Love was the dawning of the wish
To know the other when a child,
To step outside the present, which

Too rapidly is overfilled,
To trace the river to its source.
In lieu of this, Pascin resolved
To end the future without trace.

Midnight Arrives

Circadian rhythms outlast the day;
The room vibrated with the Past.
At midnight Pascin locked the door.
The room itself had cleared a space,

Then things got slightly out of hand,
As Hemingway, knocked down, had found
When Scott Fitzgerald, lost in thought,
Forgot the bell to end the round.

A Book of Days

The night of Pascin's suicide
The silver birch trees near the Dôme,
And avenues of cypresses
Stirred in their own distracted breeze.

Hermine and Lucy met and talked
And looked beyond each other's gaze
To memories now definitive
Like sheaves of drawings, numbered days.

An Empty Room

The night of Pascin's suicide
Lucy had woken from a dream,
Or something quite unlike a dream:
The world became an empty flare,

Like a railway station when the train
Has gone. She dressed, she touched her hair,
And went downstairs. The moon was high.
Its light would not confide in her.

Lucy Without Pascin

Lucy approached the water's edge
To watch night fall. A dog loped by.
A boat was leaving. All proclaimed
How irreversibly events

Outrun the visual, how all
Moves on, like harvesters in a field.
Then, as the day left dusk behind,
The world had briefly turned to gold.

At Pascin's Grave

All the Paris galleries closed.
Beneath a bright, indifferent sun,
A large crowd followed the cortège
Along the shining road. In tears

His models walked together, dressed
In long black dresses and high heels.
Musicians, barmen, waiters, all
His friends, in black, made their farewells.

Pansy

A yellow orange lies across
The valley mauves of afternoon
Like pansy petals which recall
The veined *sfumato* of Pascin,

In whose bright memory, like a flower,
She wears this pansy on her coat.
Thus Lucy and the petalled face
In wide-eyed reticence compete.

Lucy to Pascin

'The pansy, double-sided, mauve
Above and cinnamon below,
As ikat-fringed as butterflies,
Recalls dark, moonless nights with you,

Each petal watermarked with wine
With yellow-orange overlays.
And like that flower my heart is stained,
Mixed inextricably with yours.'

Forty Years On

A couple on their honeymoon
Entered a small shop on the Seine
Which advertised works by Pascin.
A frail, old lady hovered near

Some meagre sketches, shards, odd leaves.
They asked the owner if he knew
What had become of Lucy Krohg.
He pointed. 'Yes. Indeed I do.'

Conrad Satie at His Brother's Funeral

'Asked had he made his peace with God,
Thoreau replied, "I didn't know
We'd ever quarrelled." At Arcueil,
The sun stayed in to show respect;

We placed hydrangeas on the grave.
Then, as we closed the dark church doors,
I heard my brother say to God,
"I'll put on a petticoat and I'm yours."'

After the Funeral

The trolleybus which Satie took
On rainy days he liked the best,
Now in grim sunlight took Milhaud
And other friends to break the doors.

Inside they found bare furniture,
Unopened letters, broken chairs,
A table under years of dust
'Enough to make a goldfish sneeze.'

Léger Holds Forth at the Rotonde

'A painting is a glass of wine,
But a table red, *vin ordinaire*
And not champagne. Beware the air!
The light may well prevaricate

But objects don't. the world is things,
And wading out amongst their surf
It's easy in that cloud of foam
To lose the rocks, the cliffs, the turf.'

Léger Continues at the Dôme

'The Flemish painters may have caused
Much harm by introducing oils.
Before them, stood the visual world
Incised or carved in stone or wood

Or limed on frescoes, difficult,
Uncompromising. Since those days
We celebrate the blurred, the vague,
The half-lit, haystacks in a haze.'

Jean Renoir Follows His Father

'She was a flowering apple tree.
She was my mother's final gift
To my father for his *Grandes Baigneuses*.
She seemed to blossom in the house.

Each day she posed and, all the while,
She sang a sentimental air.
My father loved her. When he died,
As summer waned, I married her.'

A Walk After Rain

What has been seen as Jean Renoir's
'Aesthetic of discrepancy'
Attends the woods now after rain.
A blackbird questions and replies;

The trees shake water from their capes,
And light is scattered there like hulls.
While acorns line the shore, nearby
Beneath the oak, lie glittering shells.

Impressionism

Each morning Vollard at his door
Pretended, like his cat, to sleep
In a sunlit chair. There, bemused,
He listened when the passers-by

Passed paintings in the window. But,
In spring, intrigued by what he heard,
He did not know that, at this hour,
Wistaria dappled in the glass.

Summer

The heat was palpable. The cat
On Vollard's lap lay limp and flat.
Peach leaves as long as eucalypts
Were curled like fingers round the air.

The sky shimmered with radio waves.
Kiki cried out, 'Who wants to paint?
I'm taking off this flimsy dress.
It's just so hot. I'm feeling faint.'

Prévert Muses

'If Beauty is, as Stendhal thought,
The promise of great happiness,
Then Art should happen if we paint
Across the dappled forest floor:

I wish you happiness. Again
One might expect fresh loveliness
By seeing that the loved one wear
To your happiness across her dress.'

Jimmy Charters' Recipe for a Dry Martini

'I've had a lot of customers
Ask for an even drier dry
Martini. Here's my recipe:
First, pour some gin into a glass.

Then, with a grave, religious air,
Bend to the level of the glass,
And whisper softly, *Vermouth*. Stir
Or shake, and if desired, add ice.'

At Man Ray's Grave

A smooth stone, like his *Flat Egg*, stands.
Wild grass grows round it. Marguerites
And clumps of yellow flowers like stars
Spread in profusion, consciously,

As if they hope for photographs.
And, lightly carved, the sentiment
He so embodied: 'Unconcerned'
(He'd say) 'but not indifferent.'

Kiki Expresses Pride in Montparnasse

'Some days it seems that everyone
Who was ever here is here again:
Derain, amused by his own jokes,
Pascin, his bowler hat pulled down,

His cigarette conducting birds,
Moïse Kisling with his Tom Mix shirts,
Youki with flowers in her hair,
Desnos asleep and taking notes.'

Kiki Completes Her Roll of Honour

'McAlmon (called McAlimony)
And Kay, "her profile like a knife",
The shadows of a thousand days
Like oak trees putting out new leaves.

And some are here who, travelling,
Stepped unsuspecting from the train,
Then stayed beyond that day's delight
Like Satie savouring summer rain.'

www.ingramcontent.com/pod-product-compliance
Lightning Source LLC
Chambersburg PA
CBHW070916080526
44589CB00013B/1317